# DARK

Stories of how depression has destroyed many youths and the new remedy to depression.

Lauretta Sampson

**Content**

# INTRODUCTION

I have been depressed before, and I can say for sure that depression is not a favorable state of mind. It hurts to see countless youths from different countries die of depression or different anxiety disorders, this book was born from my depressed state, its specially for everyone out there who is finding it difficult to cope with depression, to those who want to be free from depression, to those who have been depressed before, this book will serve as a guide to easy your depression.

# 1
# THE STORY

The worst thing about being depressed is that you need help but it is so difficult to talk to someone about it because you feel they won't understand and you may be a burden to them, I was always out with my friends, I played, I smiled, I laughed with them, but deep down I was empty, I was sad for no reason, and all the happy moments were all a charade of fake joy because I felt everyone was faking their love for me. All I had in my head were negative thoughts, I felt I had lost myself and wouldn't ever be the same again, I had no motivation to do anything because I couldn't see a future for myself, and anxiety made me believe that I was alone.

I would take pills just to sleep as sleep was my only companion and waking up was a nightmare, you know how it feels when you are being served with a breakfast of sadness, loneliness, emptiness, and numbness, all a plate, they all came spontaneously but as time goes on I broke out, I could not feel anything, suicide was all I had in mind.

I followed my mum to the salon one day, it was a big plaza and the hairdressing section was on the top floor. While waiting for her to finish, I decided to get a better view from the balcony at the back of the building.

It was a quiet place with a mild sense of Nature and the view was magnificent, but all that was of no concern to me, all I could think of were negative, I burst into tears for no reason then an idea came to my head. What if I jump down and end it all, a voice In me quickly moved the motion but another voice pushed me away, the first voice was loud and gave me more reasons, while the other voice was mild and consistent, this time my tears bolstered, my frustration got the better part of me while the two voices kept battling for my soul, finally I decided to end it all I tried climbing the balcony grill when a voice shouted from behind, hey! What are you doing? I got frightened, and burst out into tears again, my mum saved me that day but she didn't give up on me.

I went through several medications and counseling and they helped me a lot but the scariest thing about my recovery process was that only I had the solution to my problem, only I can shut those voices out, only I can chase that monster out, and I believe I won the race.

## 2
## LIVING WITH DEPRESSION

Prince was 9yrs of age when he was welcomed into the world of depression, he could not tell his mum as she was battling with depression as well, ever since his dad left them for another woman, she would lock herself in the room most times drink and cry herself to sleep his dad visits occasional and leaves most times In anger as they always indulge in one argument or the order so there was no need talking to her about it. She didn't worry much about him as he was the best student in his class and his teachers acknowledged him for his excellent grades and mature personality, his mum made sure she provided all he needed but food, clothing, and shelter were not all.

It first started with a migraine which became worse after his 15th birthday, he was given Some drugs to subsidize the pain, but it didn't end there, he felt bad for his sudden poor grades in school, spent hours alone in his room and would force himself to sleep, the violence at home was more depressing so he kept his emotions unwrapped he showed no reaction to anything at home and in school because he was churned up in fear and anguish.

He broke open in his 20s and streams of depression, violence, pain, panic, and obsessions flowed out, in response to this trauma he engage in 3hrs sessions with a psychiatrist, he was able to put the panic together and was cured at a spot but he never went back to him as symptoms stopped.

2yrs later, he had another panic attack and went back to the psychiatrist, this time he was introduced to medications which helped him a bit, he didn't know what it was all he knew was that he took something In the morning that made him feel good, and something at night to help him sleep, with this he kept on seeing the psychiatrist from across the country.

The depression gradually became disruptive after some years, it pushed him into every corner of his existence and his work, relationships, and family life got affected. He went back to the psychiatrist again, he took a series of medications and different therapy sessions. prince had no idea what was wrong with him, he thought he was battling with mood swings and no one told him until he saw one of the letters from the psychiatrist, he had no idea what depression means, so he conducted a little research and had a clear picture of what he was passing through he was so relieved when he found out that he wasn't the only one passing through this pain, and truly it wasn't his him playing tricks with his mind, but from the neurologist study it was the chemistry of the brain.

Prince became so obsessed with topics related to depression, he read everything he saw about it, and later discovered that his depression was a result of an anxiety disorder called bipolar. It was a solace to see that he wasn't worthless and that it was a disease. It was a good sign of progress as he continued his research.

he had his 4th panic attack that year, and it dawned on him that he had to depend on his medications, therapy session, and most times ECT for the rest of his life, it was so painful he stayed away from everyone, he was at the point of giving up, but he didn't want to end up like most people who committed suicide.

with the help of some videos and audio podcasts from people who had the same experience, it became clear to him that the contributors to this disease are genetic inheritance, family history, stress, and misfiring of multiple body systems. he realized that the disease truly had a cure and aside from medication only he had the solution to his problem.

After tracking the causes of depression he was determined to stop the waste of life in depression he got into meditations, psychotherapy, and self-help.

P.S Let,s pause here for a while
We will continue in our other chapter

# 3
# treating depression

Today depression is the number one cause of suffering in the world of youths. so many lives have been lost, and so many families have been broken because of this disease.
but what could be the cause of this enigma, unfortunately, depression doesn't have a single cause to point out, different people have different risk factors as well as different panacea to the disease.

Major causes of depression.
**family history** - there is a 99% chance of a depressed parent raising a depressed child because the most important way of raising a child is through modeling, the child watches and learns, so there is every possibility for a depressed parent raising a depressed child. A typical example is the case of the prince in our recent chapter.

**loneliness -** take away the phone of a young adult for 2 hrs and watch their reaction, most of them can't stay without their phones, not because the phone is of great importance to them but because it has been a remedy for their loneliness and when it is been taken away they have nothing to fall bad to.
The same thing occurs with those in an intimate relationship. Everything seems beautiful and perfect but in the event of a breakup, they fall back to regrets and loneliness. This is because they saw their partner as their panacea to loneliness which is never intended to be.

**decision-making/ peer influence**. The association we keep matters a lot because they determine the decision you make and the decision you make determines the actions that follow and the actions have intended consequences. If your decisions are good, you get a good reward but if your decisions are bad you face disastrous consequences alone which could be the beginning of your depressing life. So sit up! and think straight.

**Remedy to depression**

Believe it or not, everyone does get depressed in one way or the other, it may not be that crucial or excruciating but you can not escape being depressed at some point in your life. Treating depression is a long-term process especially when it is an anxiety syndrome.

There are so many ways of treating depression, which you will soon find out, but the major remedy to depression is to avoid depression, I know you may say oh! There is no way I can avoid it, it's in me. Yes, it's in you, but there are several ways you could avoid it.

1. Meditation: our mind can be so noisy, that it could intensify depression, meditation is one way you control your mind. And when done daily and consistently you notice an inner joy in you, because your mind has mastered the act of tranquility and peace practice meditation for 30 mins daily for 6 months and you will be amazed

at the results. Depression starts from the inside, and to control it you need to start from within.

2. Exercise: I have heard people say things like, I am fit I don't need to exercise, I am very busy I don't have time for exercise, well let me be clear on this, exercising does not only keep you fit, Regular exercise helps your brain to produce a hormone called endorphins which is responsible for making us feel happy, exercise is one of the major ways to prevent and control depression

3. Relaxation technique: this includes, visualization, yoga, deep breathing, sleep, massage, etc

4. Music there
5. positive self-talk

Please note depression comes in different episodes of our lives, but those who avoid being depressed have a 45% chance of being depressed throughout their lives, while those who don't, have a higher chance.

Other methods of treating depression include

1. Therapy: this is the first treatment for depression.

2. Medications: there are different medications for depression, but these medications only numb the symptoms for a while, so it is advisable to take the medications while undergoing a therapy session.

3. Brain stimulation: this is administered in a situation where consulting a therapist and medications show no sign of improvement. It involves ECT(electroconvulsive therapy), vagus nerve stimulation, etc. this is a more severe and dangerous form of treatment.

# 4
# SELF-HELP

Let's continue our story

Prince discovered his passion for writing on topics related to depression and depressed individuals; that was where he found his innermost peace and joy. He became consistent with it, created a niche around it, and eventually created his blog.

He took control of his life, came out of his lonely shell, and decided to meet people both online and offline. He was mostly interested in people who were once depressed, they became his backbone and would motivate him more with their experience, with this, he noticed the signs of recovery, and the unpleasant thought of how worthless he is gradually died off.

A few years later, Prince became a prominent writer an author of several books on depression, and a happy father with two kids, he still experiences those symptoms reoccurring but this time he was able to control them.

Your mental health is a very important factor to consider in everything you do, and the earlier you realize it, the better it is for you.

Treating depression goes beyond medications, therapy sessions, and brain stimulation. all may work for you, but If you are not taking care of yourself and your health then you are opening the doors for depression to come in. To expect a lasting result, along with the other treatments you need to work on yourself by yourself.
This may involve
**Avoiding negative thoughts** - one of the major causes of depression boils down to how we control our emotions and thoughts.

have you ever dated a depressed person before? you will notice that they easily develop cold and negative feelings for themselves. A depressed lady calls you twice and you didn't pick her first thought would be, why didn't he pick up, he doesn't want to pick up my calls, he doesn't like me anymore, he doesn't want me anymore, and gradually she would generalize the thought, and that is where she begins to sink in depression. It all started with a negative thought. Learning to see the positive picture of everything, would help you a long way.

**The power in doing what you love** - one of the ways I prevent my depression from reoccurring is by writing, hanging out with people of like minds, and listening to music, these are what I love doing, I get this inner peace and calmness in me when I write, I feel like I am close to achieving my dreams when I hang out with good friends, music is everything to me. And these are my regular antidote for depression and it has kept me going for years, even when I fall, doing what I love most brings me back my sanity.

## 5
## Beyond depression

Happiness lies within you and depression is a friend to no man, I wish every youth out there would read this piece.
Suicide may look like the only way to solve your problem, and it may be the easiest way to stop hurting,  but I tell you today, suicide is a grave offense to you and God suicide shows how good of a loser you are. You were not born worthless neither did God put you into this world to become a wanderer or a liability. Everyone has their purpose on Earth. A purpose to serve humanity, a purpose to create an impact, you may not be loved and cared for today, but believe me, you will find more joy in caring and loving others, this is the secret of selflessness and the joy beyond depression.

According to a Neurologist study, people who have had one anxiety syndrome of depression or the other can make better decisions in the future, most of them find their purpose after a dark tunnel of depression because many of life's failures are people who did not realize how close they were to success before they gave up. Being depressed is not the end of the world, there is a beautiful and more prosperous life after depression.

**Conclusion**

- Parents try to raise their kids away from violence, no matter how bad the situation could be, children should be kept away from violence.
- Your friends can make or mare you, they can as well influence the decisions you make. And the decision you make will determine if you will be depressed or not choose wisely.
- Try not to place people or things as an antidote for loneliness
- Self-help is the key, find your passion find joy.

Thank you for reading this book,
I urge you to keep fighting, it's not always as easy as it seems, always remember that the end is always worth the struggle.
Stay positive stay happy.

www.ingramcontent.com/pod-product-compliance
Lightning Source LLC
LaVergne TN
LVHW080600160826
845677LV00010B/1934
*9798361195145*